SOCCER

Loans are up to 28 days. Fines are charged if items are not returned by the due date. Items can be renewed at the Library, via the internet or by telephone up to 3 times. Items in demand will not be renewed.

Please use a bookmark

arrett

ieris

Date for return

Check out our online catalogue to see what's in stock, or to renew or reserve books.

www.birmingham.gov.uk/libcat

www.birmingham.gov.uk/libraries

Birmingham City Council

Birmingham
Libraries

SPORTS SKILLS

Cricket	Netball
Gymnastics	Rugby Union
Hockey	Soccer
Judo	Tennis

Photographs by Action Plus, except pages 15 and 21 (left) by Bob Thomas Sports Photography, page 23 by Sally and Richard Greenhill and page 25 by Norman Barrett
Illustrations by James Robins and Drawing Attention
Consultant Don Howe, Chelsea Football Club Coach, formerly coached the England soccer team

This edition published in 1995 by
Wayland (Publishers) Ltd

First published in 1993 by
Wayland (Publishers) Ltd
61 Western Road, Hove
East Sussex BN3 1JD, England

British Library Cataloguing in Publication Data
Barrett, Norman
    Soccer. - (Sports Skills Series)
    I. Title II. Jefferis, David
    III. Robins, James IV. Series
    796.334

HARDBACK ISBN 0-7502-0699-3

PAPERBACK ISBN 0-7502-1697-2

DTP by The Design Shop
Printed and bound in Italy by G. Canale & C.S.p.A., Turin

Contents

Introduction

Soccer is the most popular sport in the world. It is played in every country, and big competitions such as the World Cup are watched on TV by millions of people. Traditionally a game for boys and men, soccer is now played more and more by girls and women.

The official name of soccer is 'association football'. In Britain, where it first began, and in many other places, it is often known simply as football. Whatever you call it, you can enjoy soccer as a 'kick-about' in the park or any other open space, or you can play a full 11-a-side match on a properly marked-out pitch.

△ There is plenty of bodily contact in soccer, as opposing players strive to win the ball.

In soccer, as in most sports, you most easily develop your skills when you are young. Some people have a natural flair, but even the best footballers have got where they are by practising.

There are many skills in the game. You learn to kick the ball with both feet, to pass in different ways and to shoot at goal. You learn to control the ball with various parts of your body, and to play the ball with your head, a skill unique to soccer. Special skills include dribbling and goalkeeping.

You can practise soccer skills by yourself, with a partner or in small groups. 'Small-sided games', often with special rules, are excellent for practice. The danger of playing too many full-scale matches is that you have little chance to sharpen your basic skills. You don't get enough touches of the ball.

△ Goalmouth action from a professional match. Players jump to reach a high ball, but the goalkeeper manages to punch it clear.

Getting started

You do not need a lot of expensive equipment to play soccer. Footwear is most important, and you should take great care when buying your boots. When you try them on, do the laces up and walk around. They must fit comfortably, neither too tight nor too loose. Never buy a pair just because they look good.

Take good care of your football boots. Undo the laces properly before taking them off. After use, knock off any loose mud, wipe them over and stuff them with paper. Let them dry naturally overnight before polishing them.

A pair of strong trainers is ideal for practice indoors or on hard surfaces. A deep tread on the soles will give you extra grip.

Other equipment includes: a shirt, shin-guards, socks, shorts and support underwear.

Kit and equipment

Boots with screw-in studs

Shin-guards

It is worth paying a little more for boots with screw-in studs, Boots with moulded studs are cheaper, but are unsuitable for playing when a pitch is muddy. You need to screw in longer studs for such conditions. Shin-guards are compulsory for official matches. Lightweight shin-guards are comfortable, and there is no reason not to wear them whenever your shins are likely to come into contact with studs.

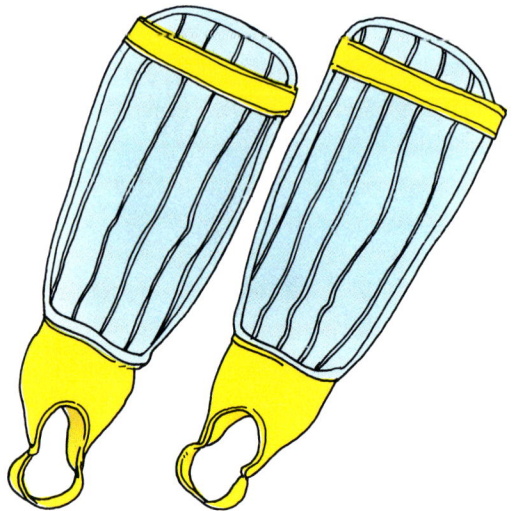

△ Coaching soccer at a summer camp. You can get started at school, and many professional clubs run classes for promising young players.

You can play for your school, and there are national competitions for junior sides. But it is more important to develop your skills at a young age than to take part in too many full-scale matches.

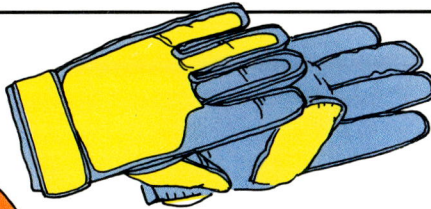

Goalkeeper's gloves are designed to give good grip and to protect the hands and wrists.

Young footballers do not need a full-size football (No. 5). Size 3 or 4 is adequate. If you have your own ball, wipe it dry after use.

Rules and refereeing

Soccer is a simple game to play, but some of the rules lead to arguments. The referee, who is helped by the two linesmen, sometimes has a difficult job in applying the rules fairly, but together they do their best.

So the first and most important rule of football is to accept the referee's decisions. Never argue or show dissent in any way. Not only could you be cautioned or sent off, but it is not in the spirit of the game.

It is particularly difficult for the referee to apply the law relating to fouls. Offences range from kicking an opponent to handling the ball. But the referee must judge whether an offence is intentional.

The referee may allow play to continue to prevent a side gaining from committing an offence, but has to decide immediately. This is called the 'advantage' rule.

Referee's signals

The referee shows decisions by blowing a whistle and using signals.
1 Direct free-kick - hand indicates direction.
2 Hand points to the ground - a goal-kick or a penalty-kick, depending on where the hand is pointing.
3 Indirect free-kick - hand held up.
4 Play on - the referee has seen an offence but allows the team in possession of the ball to play on.
5 Official caution - the referee takes the player's name and shows a yellow card. Showing a red card indicates a sending-off.

Offside

Here are some basic examples of how the offside law works. The defending players are denoted by white figures, the attackers by blue.

1 Attacker **A** passes to team-mate **B**. **B** is nearer the defending goal line than the ball as team-mate **A** plays the ball. **B** is offside because there is only one opponent closer to the goal line.

2 This time, as **A** passes the ball, there are two defenders closer to the goal line than **B1**. So **B1** is not offside, and can move forward to collect the pass (**B2**).

3 Player **A** shoots and scores, but **B** is offside and interfering with play by distracting the goalkeeper. **B** might not be interfering on purpose, but the referee should rule 'no goal'.

4 Here, **B** is not offside when **A** passes the ball because it is closer to the goal line than **B**.

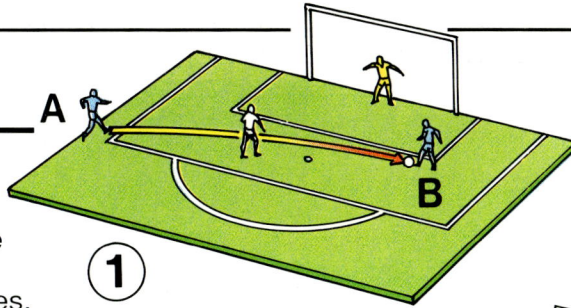

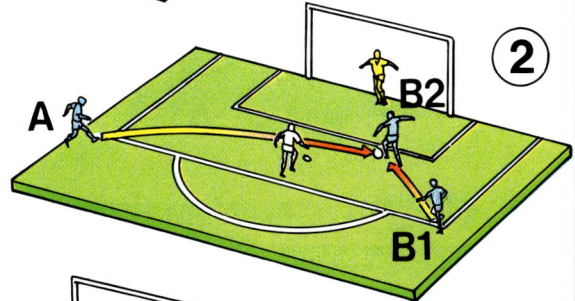

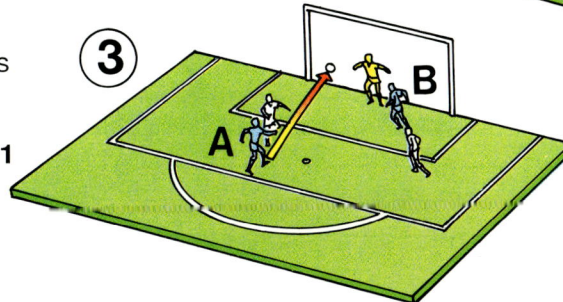

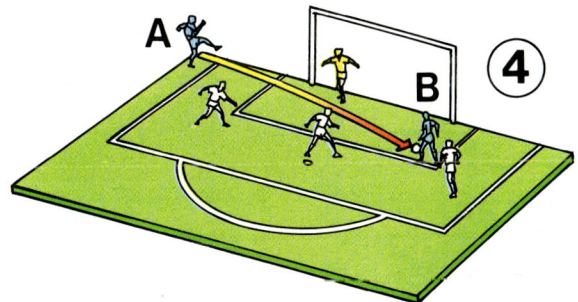

Another rule that causes controversy is the offside law. When a team-mate plays the ball, players are offside if they are closer to the other side's goal line than the ball, unless there are at least two opponents level with them or between them and the goal line at the moment the ball was played. Players cannot be offside in their own half or direct from a throw-in, corner-kick or goal-kick.

It is a linesman's job to spot offsides, and raise a flag to alert the referee. The difficulty for officials is that offside is not an offence if the referee judges that the player is not interfering with play or an opponent or seeking to gain an advantage.

Building blocks

Passes are the building blocks of football. You can make long or short passes, passes with your foot, head, chest or any other part of your body except your hands and arms. Teams build up attacks with passes, and make goal-scoring opportunities. The idea of passing is to give the ball to a team-mate who is in a better position than yourself to use it.

Most passes are made with the foot - the inside or outside of the foot, the side of the foot, the instep (the part under the laces) or even the sole or heel. With practice, you can 'chip' a ball over opponents, 'bend' it round them or 'cross' it from the wing to the goalmouth so that it swings away from their goalkeeper.

◁ Making even a short pass with the side of your foot calls for great care. It is worth developing good habits from an early age - eyes on the ball, arms out for balance and head over the ball.

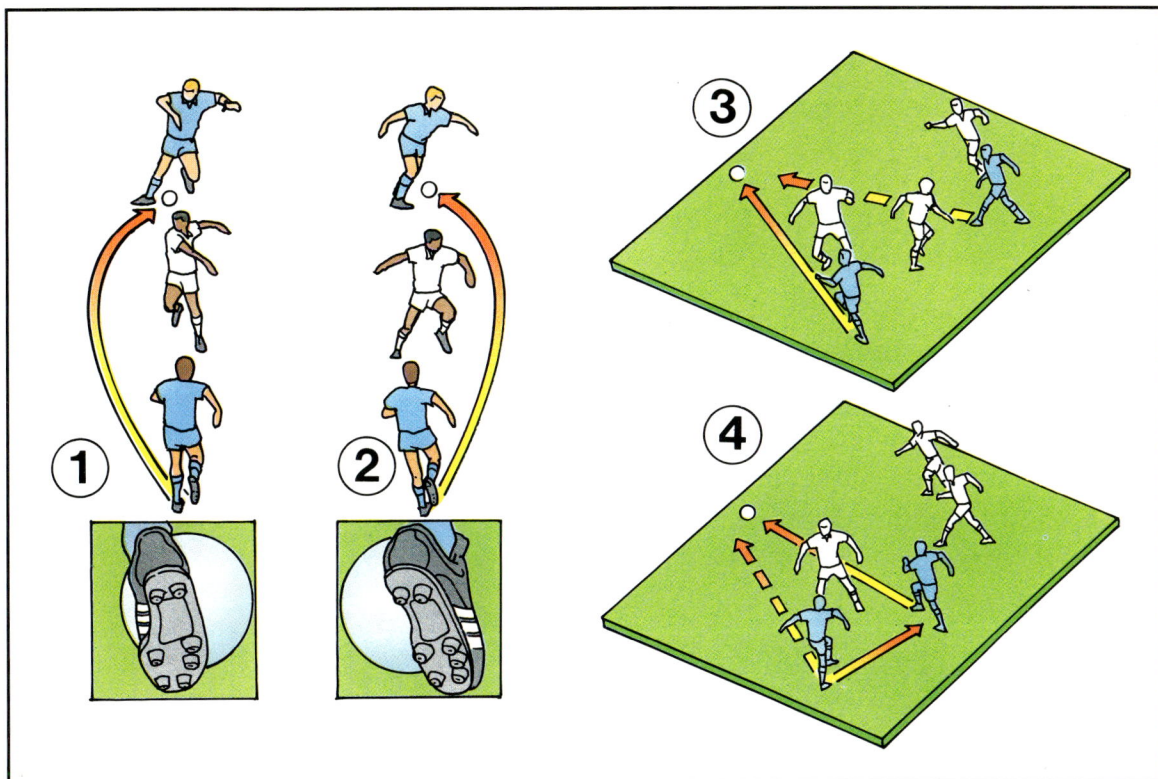

A good pass has to be accurate, but also needs to be hit with the right 'weight', or strength. Played too hard, a pass might be difficult for your team-mate to control. Without enough weight, it might be intercepted by an opponent.

The timing of a pass may also be crucial. First-time passes (such as a 'wall pass') are more likely to split an opposing defence. But sometimes you have to hold on to the ball while a team-mate runs into a good position to accept a pass.

The most important factor in teamwork is support for the player in possession. Making yourself available for a pass is called 'running off the ball'. The more options players have, the easier it is for them to make a telling pass. And even if you do not receive a pass, you will take up the attention of at least one opponent.

△ **1** Hitting the ball with the outside of the foot to 'bend' it round an opponent.
2 Striking the ball with the inside of the foot bends it the other way. In addition, to chip the ball, you lean back slightly and make contact with the bottom half of the ball.
3 Running off the ball involves moving into position when a team-mate has the ball in order to receive a pass.
4 The wall pass, or 'one-two', is a movement between two players - one uses the other as a 'wall' to bounce a pass off.

Controlling the ball

Quick control of the ball is vital in football. Unless you are making a first-time pass, a clearance or an attempt at goal, you need to bring the ball under your command.

You can control the ball with any part of your body except, of course, your hands or arms. The idea is to cushion the ball, to take the pace off it. You aim to put the ball in the best position for your next touch, whether you intend to pass, shoot or run with it. At the same time, you must keep the ball away from your opponents.

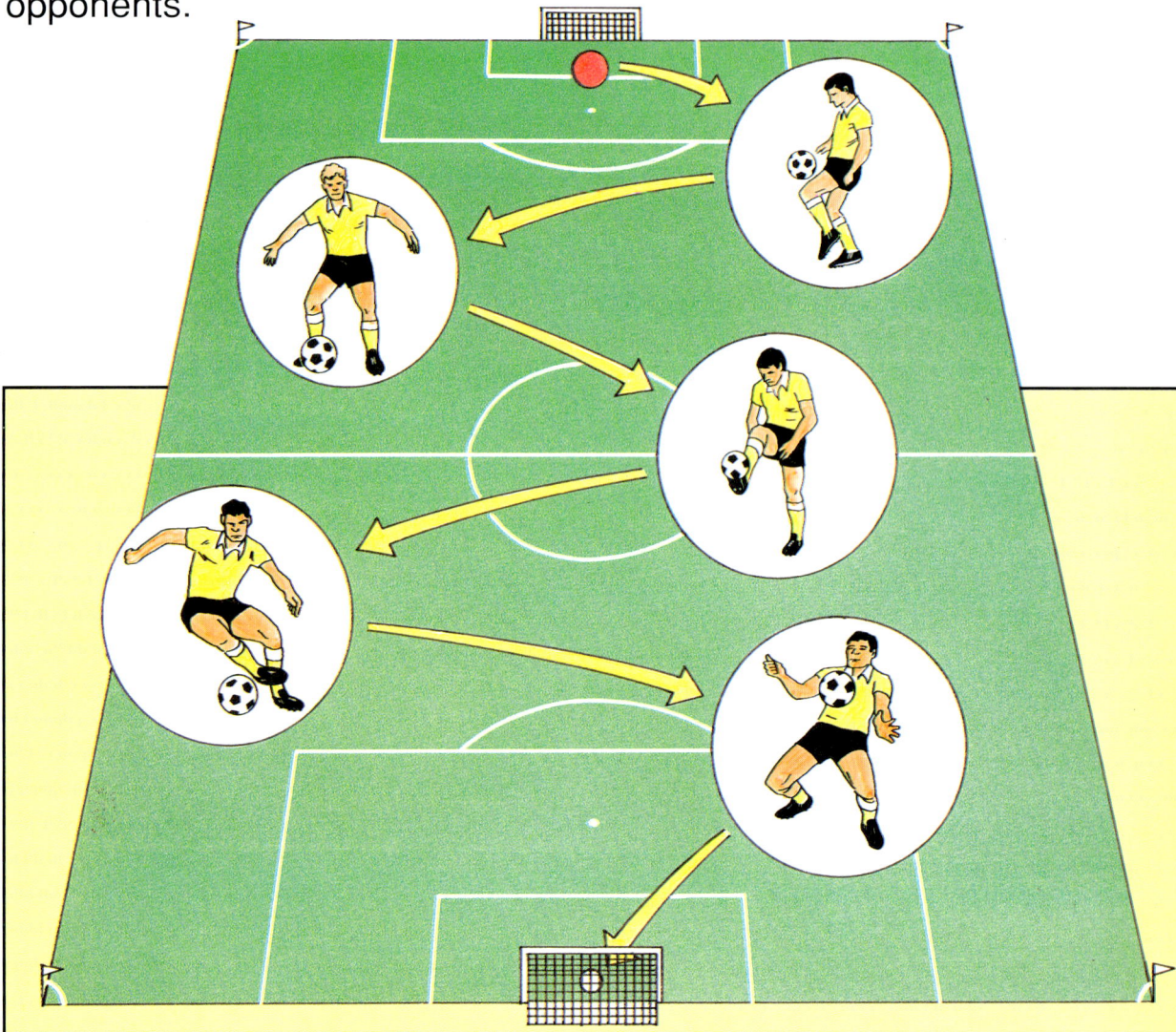

Masters of the pitch

Players usually control the ball with foot, thigh or chest. Whichever part you use, withdraw it slightly just as you are about to make contact. If you need to push the ball forward, as when running, you can cushion it by just letting it hit you in the midriff, the area between chest and legs.

1 Thigh control enables you to bring a high ball down to your feet. The thigh is the best cushion of all.

2 Side of foot is used to take the pace off a ball rolling along the ground.

3 Instep is used like a hand to pluck a dropping ball out of the air.

4 Inside or outside of foot is used to squeeze the ball against the ground in the direction you want to run.

5 The chest is used for a high ball coming at you.

△ The German striker Jurgen Klinsmann is being tightly marked by his Italian opponent. The ball is coming to Klinsmann in the air and he is about to use his chest to control it. He can drop the ball straight down to his feet, ready for a quick pass pass to a team-mate. Or he could surprise his marker by half-turning and chesting the ball down at an angle to get past.

Using your head

When you head the ball, it's best to make contact with your forehead. Keep your eyes on the ball as you jump, and hit it squarely with your forehead. If you let the ball drop on to the top of your head, you will probably get hurt. The only exception to this is when you allow a ball coming towards you to glance off the top of your head in order to deflect it.

Heading the ball in attack and defence calls for different skills. In attack, you may power a header at goal. This is especially difficult for the keeper to save if directed downwards. In defence, when your own goal is threatened, it is usually best to clear the ball with a high, long header.

Power heading

1 Correct timing is vital in heading. Like catching a ball thrown long and high, you need to position yourself first, and this calls for good judgement.

2 Keep your eyes on the ball and meet it at the top of your jump, with your arms held out in front of you for poise and balance as you draw your head back, ready to strike.

3 'Punch' your head through your arms and strike the ball with your forehead. To head the ball downwards, your head should be higher than the ball on contact.

△ It may seem difficult at first, but you should keep your eyes on the ball when heading it.

Shooting for goal

Goal-scoring calls for alertness in front of the goal. Anticipation and the ability to think and move quickly are vital when trying to get past defenders.

Most goals are scored with 'prod-ins' and deflections. But a powerful, accurate shot is a dangerous weapon in the armoury of any attacking player.

For power, you hit the ball with your instep. To prevent the ball rising too high, keep your head down as you make contact. If the ball is on the ground, place your non-kicking foot alongside the ball.

Good goalkeepers come out to narrow the angle when an opponent is about to shoot. So learn how to bend the ball, hitting it off-centre, and practise 'volleying', or striking the ball off the ground, and shooting with your weaker foot, too.

△ With your non-kicking foot at the side of the ball and your head down (**1**), make contact with your instep (**2**) and follow through (**3**).

◁ Denmark's Michael Laudrup (to the right in the picture) shoots for goal. This is a fine illustration of how to strike a ball. But he is setting a poor example by not wearing shin-guards, which is now illegal.

The art of dribbling

Running at the opposing defence with the ball creates problems for them, especially if you can beat a player or two. Others have to cover the danger, giving your team-mates chances to break free.

Keeping the ball under close control and taking it past opponents is called 'dribbling'. Half the art of dribbling is knowing when to release the ball, passing to a team-mate in a good position or taking a shot at goal. Practise controlling the ball with the inside and outside of both feet while moving at speed. Try feinting movements, such as dropping your shoulder, swerving or changing pace - anything to confuse opponents and disturb their balance.

△ Dutch star Ruud Gullit leaves a defender sprawling as he takes the ball past, having sent the defender the wrong way.

Keeping goal

Goalkeeping is a special craft and calls for skills entirely different from those of the ten outfield players. Safe handling is a keeper's most valuable gift. It does not matter how agile and acrobatic you are between the posts, if the ball does not stick when you attempt to catch a cross or a shot, you will give away goals.

Sharp reflexes are also important. A keeper must be able to deal with shots and headers coming in at all angles, especially if the ball is deflected. A keeper also needs to be fairly tall in order to cover all corners of the goal. Other goalkeeping assets include a strong kick and an accurate throw to start up attacks.

Goalkeeping skills

1 Fielding a low ball - legs behind the line of the ball.
2 Diving to save - one hand behind the ball, the other quickly round to clasp it.
3 and **4** Catching a high cross and bringing it down safely to the chest.
5 The keeper comes out of goal to narrow the target for an oncoming attacker. This calls for good judgement, not only of the angles, but in timing. Coming out too soon might allow opponents to chip the ball over your head. Too late, and they have plenty of space to score either side of you.

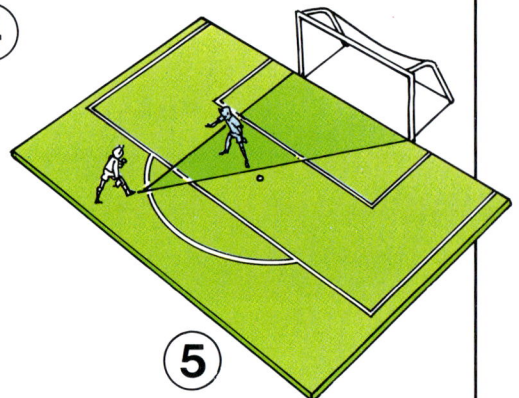

A goalkeeper should be master of the penalty area, organizing the defence and calling out instructions when necessary. As a keeper, you may handle the ball only in the penalty area, but must not do so if the ball is passed to you from the foot of a team-mate.

You need a good footballing brain - to know whether to stay in goal or come out and go for the ball. You might have to dive in to grab the ball among a forest of thrashing legs, or race out of the penalty area to break up a sudden attack. For such excursions, you need speed off the mark, confidence and courage.

△ Keepers need speed and agility to dive for shots to the corners of the goal.

Special skills

A football team is made up of players with a wide range of abilities, from scoring goals to saving them. Ball-winning is most important and calls for special skills. Tackling is one way to win the ball, either face-to-face with an opponent - the block tackle - or from the side. But it is much better to anticipate a pass or force an error.

Keeping yourself between an opposing ball-carrier and your goal is called 'jockeying'. It gives your team-mates time to get back and might force your opponent into a false move, allowing you to win possession.

Other special soccer skills include throwing in, screening the ball and, with your back to goal, turning with the ball to beat an opponent.

◁ You need good timing to make a sliding tackle. The idea is to push the ball to safety, either to a team-mate or out of play. If you miss, you will either put yourself out of play or foul your opponent.

△ Screening the ball - shielding it with legs and body - makes it difficult for an opponent to challenge for it. It should become a habit whenever you have possession and want more time on the ball, whether dribbling or waiting to pass.

△ The throw-in must be made with both hands and from behind your head. Part of both feet must be on the ground and they must not stick out over the touchline. Some players can throw the ball from the touchline into their opponents' goalmouth.

Turning with the ball

Turning with the ball is a skill used mostly by forwards with their back to goal.

1 As the ball comes to you, you feint to go one way.

2 Then you turn in the opposite direction, taking the ball in one movement past the player who is marking you.

Training games 1

The best way to practise and develop your skills is to take part in small-sided games. You can play from one-a-side to six- or seven-a-side, with all kinds of variations.

With just a few players involved, you receive the ball much more often. Small-sided games can be designed to develop particular skills. There are special games for goalkeepers, and all the outfield skills can be sharpened up in games specially devised for the purpose.

Most training games are played on small areas of the pitch, such as a penalty area, and have special rules. In some training games, for example, you may be allowed only one touch of the ball when you receive it, before you must pass or shoot.

◁ Small-sided games are usually competitive. Five-a-side football is played with smaller goals and on a small pitch or court, and now has its own official rules.

You can practise by yourself, keeping the ball in the air without letting it bounce, or shooting at a target on a wall. You might try keeping the ball up with your head five times. When you have achieved this, try doing it 10 times, and so on.

Set your targets higher as you improve. See how many times out of 10 you can hit that target on the wall, first with one foot, then with the other. Try using different parts of your foot to play the ball.

Kick or throw the ball against the wall and control it as it bounces back to you with various parts of your body. Walls are good for heading practice, too. You can try scoring headers, defensive headers or just keep heading the ball against the wall.

△ Everyone gets more touches of the ball in small-sided games.

Training games 2

◁ In this game for four players, several skills are brought into play. Attackers make first-time passes, especially one-twos, and shots at goal. For defenders, there is closing down and tackling.

The game, 3 minutes each way, is played two-a-side on a 20 m x 15 m area, with a goal at each end.

The team in possession attacks. One of the defenders plays as goalkeeper. The teams change roles as soon as one side scores, the ball goes out of play or the defenders win the ball. The new attackers must give the defenders time to get a player in goal.

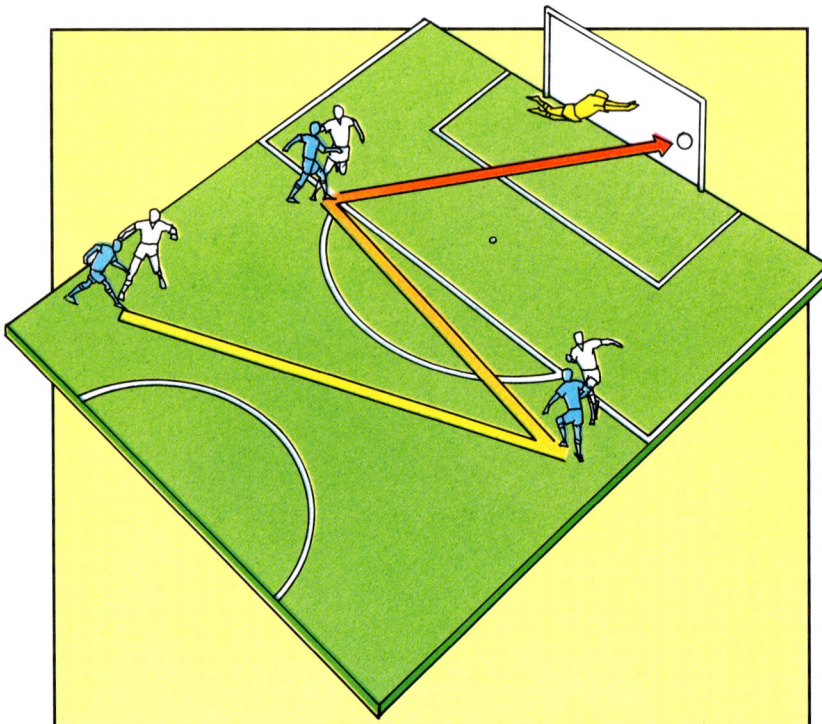

◁ This game for seven, played three-a-side with a neutral goalkeeper, is good for shooting practice in realistic situations. First-time passing, defending and shot-stopping also come into it.

The area is a penalty box extended to the half-way line, about 40 m x 55 m. Play lasts 20 minutes.

The teams attack the same goal, and, on gaining the ball, a team must make at least two passes before they can score. The keeper, on gaining possession, must throw the ball out to the player farthest from goal.

△ A good practice for keepers is to use cones for deflecting shots.

▷ This six-a-side game is mainly for developing heading skills. It is played on a quarter pitch, about 60 m x 35 m, with a goal at each end. Each side has a keeper, and the game is 10 minutes each way.

The team in possession attacks by alternate heading and throwing (catching the ball first). The attackers may make two consecutive headers, but not throws. Goals may be scored only with headers.

Defenders may intercept only with their heads, and then the first team to grab the ball wins possession.

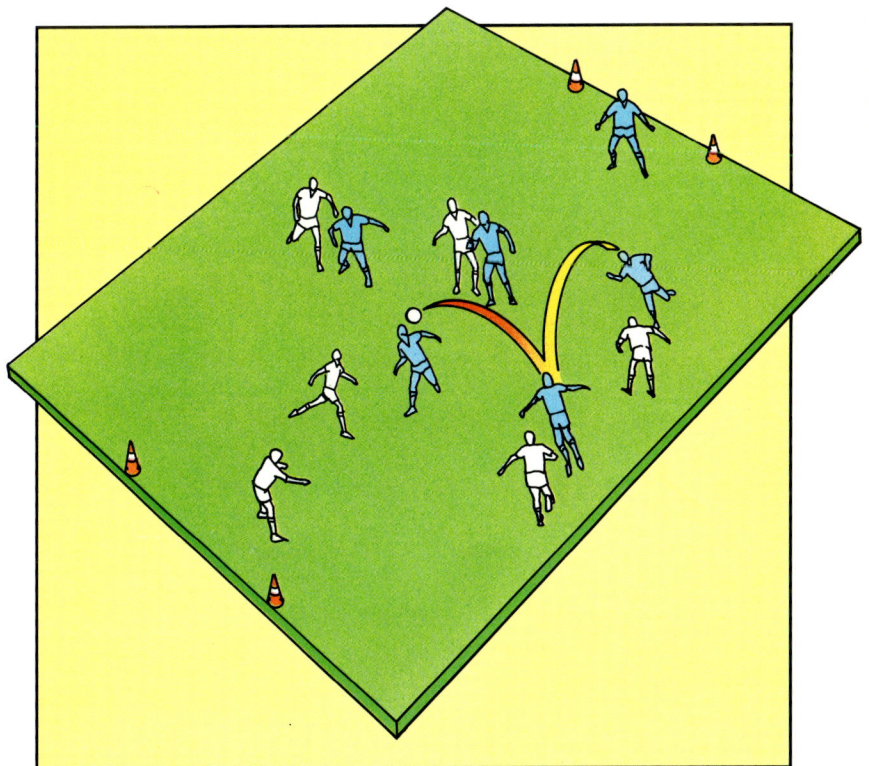

Tactics and teamwork 1

In soccer, play moves quickly from end to end, and success depends on good teamwork allied to individual skills.

The outfield players may be divided into three groups - defence, midfield and attack. But these are loose labels. The guiding principle of modern soccer is: 'In possession, you are all attackers, when the other side has the ball you are defenders.'

Teams usually play with a certain formation of outfield players, such as four defenders, three in midfield and three in attack. This is known as 4-3-3.

Some teams use a 'sweeper', a loose player behind the defence with no specific marking duties. The formation then might be 1-4-3-2, with the '1' referring to the sweeper.

Team formations

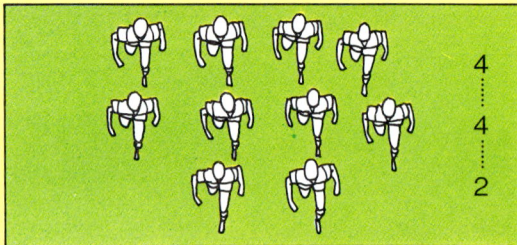

△ This is a 4-4-2 formation. The back four play a zonal defence with twin strikers, or striker and winger up front.

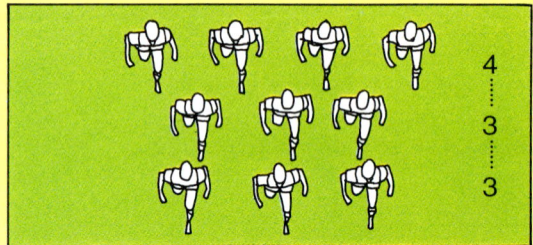

△ In 4-3-3, there is again a four-man zonal defence, but, with three up front, more emphasis on attack.

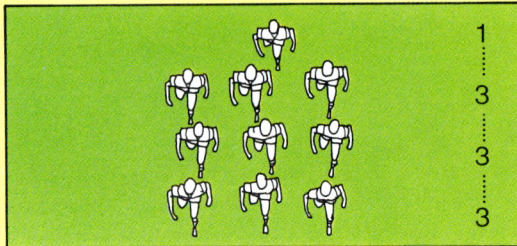

△ The 1-3-3-3 line-up is a version of the sweeper system, with three defenders marking man for man.

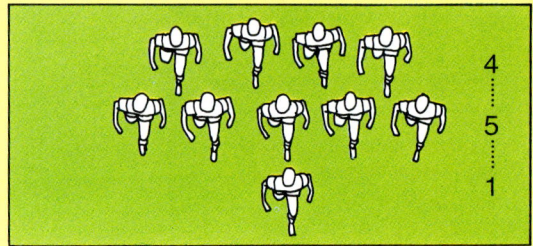

△ In this 4-5-1 line-up, a single striker is supported by most of the five midfielders pushing forward on runs.

Playing plans

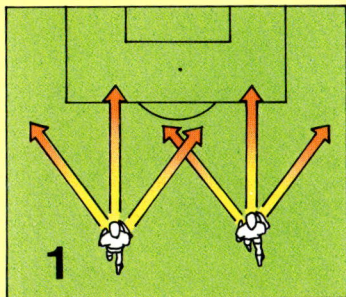

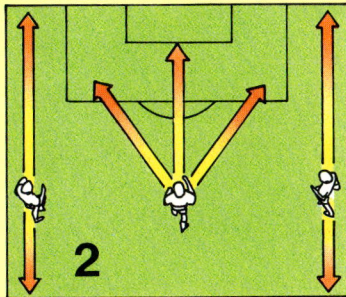

Attack
1 Twin strikers, playing without wingers, make runs to the wings as well as attacking through he middle.
2 Some teams play two wingers with a central striker. The wingers keep defenders out wide.

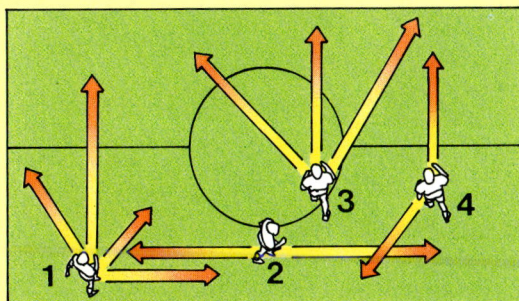

Midfield
Several types of players operate in midfield. Most teams have a play-maker (**1**), or midfield general, to dictate play and set up attacks. An anchorman (**2**) breaks up opposing attacks by winning the ball. A through runner (**3**) bursts to the front at every opportunity. A withdrawn winger (**4**) attacks and defends along the touchline.

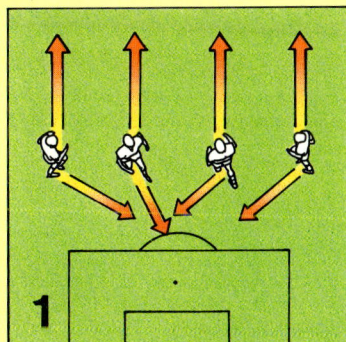

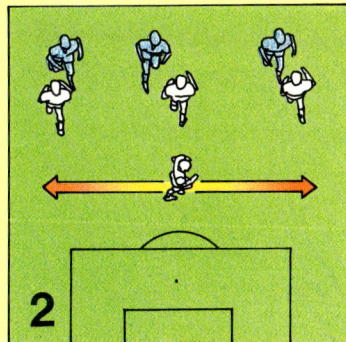

Defence
1 In zonal defence, each defender covers a strip of the pitch and marks or challenges any attacker who enters it.
2 A sweeper operates behind man-for-man markers, picking up those balls played through or over them.

Defenders either mark 'man for man', following their designated 'opponent' around the pitch, or play a 'zonal' defence. In this, they are responsible for areas of the pitch rather than players.

Midfield players link defence with attack. They have various functions. Some are there to win the ball, others to use it. And there are midfielders whose chief job is to make forward runs and steal up into the opposing goalmouth to get on the end of a through ball or cross.

In attack, strikers operate up front, often in pairs. Wingers patrol the flanks and try to get round the defence to make crosses.

Tactics and teamwork 2

The system a team adopts often depends on the skills of the players available. Soccer is a tactical game, and a manager's plans may count for nothing if the opposition does something unexpected. Managers can plan to make the most of their side's strengths, and exploit the opposition's weaknesses, but once the game starts, anything can happen.

There are certain aspects of play, however, that can be planned and rehearsed. These are the set-pieces, or 'restarts', which occur after the ball goes out of play or the game is stopped by the referee. The chief attacking set-pieces are free-kicks around the opposing penalty area, corner-kicks and, to a lesser extent, throw-ins. Players also practise defending against free-kicks and corner-kicks.

△ The heads go up for a corner-kick. The big players from both sides - central defenders and strikers - pack the goalmouth before corner-kicks, and the keeper needs good judgement to decide whether to go for the ball or stay on his line.

Note the defenders (numbers 5 and 10) covering the corners of the goal, which the keeper cannot easily reach.

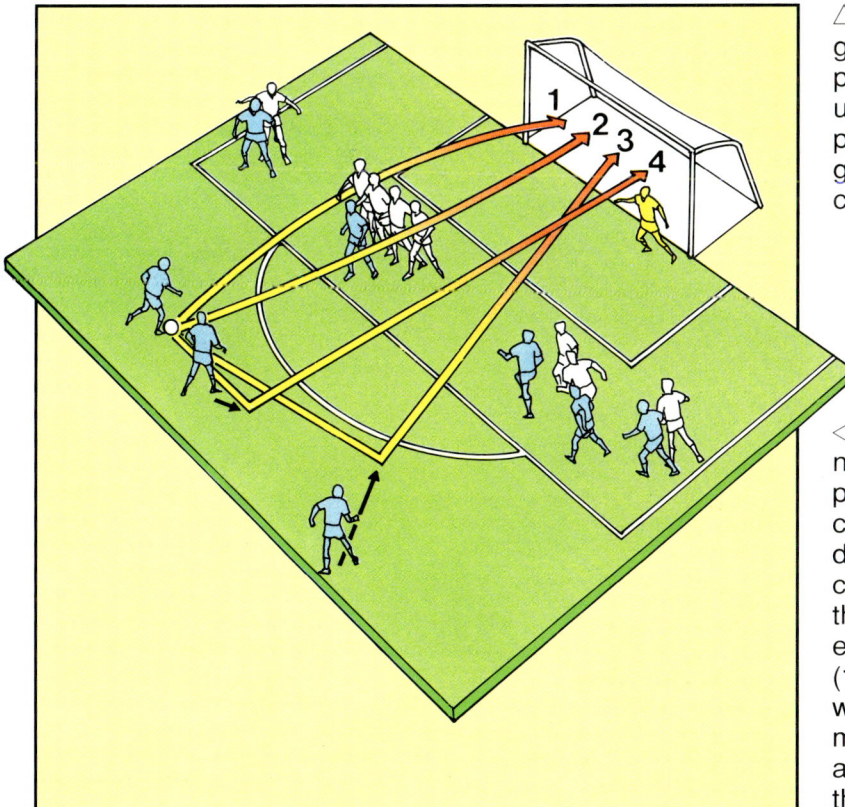

△ Free-kicks in front of goal are dangerous set-pieces. The defending side usually line up a 'wall' of players to protect half the goal, while the keeper covers the other half.

◁ Every side should have a number of well-rehearsed plans for taking free-kicks close to the penalty box. A defensive wall lines up to cut off attempts at 'bending' the ball, but some free-kick experts can still bend it past (1) or chip it over (2) the wall. Passing to a team-mate to change the angle is another good way to beat the wall (3 and 4).

Glossary

Bending the ball
Striking the ball on the side so that it swerves.

Chip
A lofted pass or shot.

Closing down
Advancing on opposing ball-carriers to stop them making good use of the ball.

Cross
A pass made from the wing into the goalmouth.

Dissent
Showing disagreement with the decision of an official.

First-time pass
A pass made with the first touch.

Goalmouth
The area in front of the goal.

Instep
The upper part of the foot, under the laces.

Jockeying
Holding up an opposing ball-carrier and steering him or her into a less dangerous position, while allowing your team-mates to regroup and cover.

Man-for-man marking
A system in which defenders are each responsible for one opponent, sticking to them wherever they go.

Midfield general
See Play-maker.

One-two
A passing movement in which one player passes the ball to a team-mate and runs into position for an immediate return pass, beating one or more opponents on the way. Also called a 'wall pass'.

Play-maker
A midfield player, also called the 'midfield general', who controls his or her side's pattern of play, setting up their attacks.

Running off the ball
Making a move, either to position yourself for a pass or to draw opponents out of position.

Screening
Shielding the ball with body or legs to make it difficult for an opponent to challenge for it or tackle you.

Set-piece
Plan for attack when a team is restarting the game with a free-kick, corner-kick or throw-in.

Small-sided game
Practice game for a small number of players aimed at bringing out certain skills.

Striker
A front player whose main job is scoring goals.

Support underwear
Protection garments worn under the shorts or (for girls) the shirt.

Sweeper
A player in some formations whose job is to cover fellow defenders, usually from behind.

Volley
A shot made by hitting the ball when it is off the ground.

Wall
A defensive line of players set up to block opposing free-kicks.

Wall pass   *See* One-two.

Winger
An attacking player who operates mainly along the sides, or 'wings', of the pitch.

Withdrawn winger
Midfield player who operates as a winger but also with marking and tackling duties.

Books to read

Soccer (Granada Guides series), Norman Barrett (Granada, 1983)
Soccer (How to Play series), Liz French (Jarrold, 1991)
Soccer (Play the Game series), Ken Goldman and Peter Dunk
   Ward Lock, 1988)
Soccer, the Skills of the Game, Tony Book (Crowood Press, 1989)
Take up Soccer, Mike Smith (Springfield Books, 1989)

For teachers and coaches:
Skilful Soccer, Stephen Ford and Colin Woffinden
   (Guinness, 1991)
*Referees' Chart and Players' Guide to the Laws of Association
   Football,* (Pan Books, revised annually)

Index